NORTH AMERICAN INDIAN ART

ERNA SIEBERT · WERNER FORMAN

NORTH AMERICAN INDIAN ART

MASKS, AMULETS, WOOD CARVINGS AND CEREMONIAL DRESS FROM THE NORTH-WEST COAST

PAUL HAMLYN

INTRODUCTION BY ERNA SIEBERT
NOTES ON THE PLATES BY E. SIEBERT AND N. SMIRNOVA
PHOTOGRAPHY BY WERNER FORMAN
TRANSLATION BY PHILIPPA HENTGÈS
GRAPHIC DESIGN BY BEDŘICH FORMAN
DESIGNED AND PRODUCED BY ARTIA FOR
PAUL HAMLYN LTD
DRURY HOUSE, RUSSELL STREET, LONDON WC2
© 1967 BY ARTIA
PRINTED IN CZECHOSLOVAKIA
S 2016

LIST OF CONTENTS

ACKNOWLEDGEMENTS

The objects are reproduced by kind permission of the Museum of Anthropology and Ethnography of the Academy of Sciences, Leningrad (Illustrations 1-13, 16-20, 25-29, 31-35; Plates 1-23, 29-58, 60-76, 82-101), and the Anthropological Museum of the Lomonosov State University, Moscow (Illustrations 14-15, 21-24, 30; Plates 24-28, 59, 77-81, 102-107).

1. WOODEN MASK IN THE FORM OF A HUMAN FACE.

THE ART OF THE INDIAN TRIBES LIVING along the North-West Coast of America has become more widely known in the past few years, through a number of articles and books devoted to the culture of the American Indians as a whole. However, the culture of the North-West Coastal tribes still remains the limited domain of the ethnographer and the collector of primitive carving and sculpture. It has mainly been studied from exhibits in American and European museums, especially the latter, to which most of the early collections found their way. A particularly fine collection of pieces that Russian seafarers and explorers brought back to St Petersburg, and which is now in the Leningrad Museum of Anthropology and Ethnography, provides rich evidence of the culture of the Tlingit tribes who lived along the North-West Coast. As the Soviet ethnographer Sternberg has said, this complete and valuable collection is 'the earliest and most authentic of all collections of this type.'[1] It was built up when Russian America (1741–1867) comprised Alaska, the North-West Coast (down to approximately a latitude of 55°N) and the Aleutian chain of islands, as well as one or two other islands in the eastern part of the Bering Sea.

The Bering and Chirikov expedition of 1741 and 1742 paved the way for the scientific study of the lands, seas and islands of the North Pacific area. At that time isolated facts about the 'peoples of America' began to appear in Russian scientific journals. The Billings and Sarychev expedition in 1790 found 'Americans' (probably Tlingits) on the mainland, a little to the south of Mount Elias (60°N).

Most of the ships that sailed the North Pacific towards the end of the eighteenth century belonged to traders seeking valuable furs. Of Captain George Dixon, who set sail in 1786, La Perouse wrote that 'he did not intend to make discoveries, but sought to acquire cheaply the finest furs which he could sell to the Chinese at high prices.' Only a few seafarers set out with the idea of exploration. The most famous expeditions are those of James Cook (1778), La Perouse (1786) and Vancouver (1792–1794). Many navigators of that time knew of the Russian expeditions. La Perouse went to explore the places 'undiscovered by Captain Cook and about which the Russian and Spanish navigators have given no indication.'

Many accounts of voyages began to be published. Although the sailors and traders did not establish lasting relations with the natives, almost all these books describe meetings with various Indian tribes in the North-West Coast area. While Cook and Vancouver were the first Europeans to meet the more southerly tribes living along the coast (Nootkas, Kwakiutls and Haidas),

---

[1] An equally fine collection, though rather small, is to be found in the Anthropological Museum of Lomonosov State University, Moscow.

2. WOODEN MASK OF A WOMAN WEARING A LABRET.

3. SHAMAN'S FRONTAL MASK OF CARVED WOOD.

4. WOODEN FRONTAL MASK. SEE ALSO PLATES 18, 19.

the Russians were the first to discover the Tlingits, the most northerly North-West Coast Indians.

The development of the territory of America was closely bound up with the round-the-world voyages of the Russian seamen. Almost all the expeditions set out to establish trading bases for the Russian American Company and some of them even wintered at these bases. Their log-books give detailed accounts of the Tlingits, the Athapascans, the Aleuts and the Eskimos. The first Russians to voyage round the world were Captain Krusenstern and Captain Lisiansky, who sailed in the *Nadezhda* (Hope) and the *Neva* from 1803 to 1806. Their accounts give all kinds of information about the customs of the North Pacific islanders and the tribes of the coastal area. Lisiansky gives one of the most complete ethnographical descriptions of the time about the native peoples encountered by the expedition. Equally invaluable material is to be found in the logs of Golovnin's voyage on the *Kamchatka* (1817–1819) and Andrei Lazarev's voyage on the *Ladoga* (1822–1824). Perhaps the most detailed of all these accounts though was written by Admiral Lütke (1817-1819), and published between 1834 and 1836.

From roughly 1820 to 1850, ethnographers began to study the people of this region. The Russian American colonies were then visited by such brilliant explorers as Khlebnikov, Wrangel, Veniaminov, Voznesensky and Zagoskin. The accounts of their day-to-day observations during expeditions to different parts of the area provided the first scientific data about the native population.

These ethnographical descriptions of the early nineteenth century are particularly invaluable, for the life of the Indians had not then been influenced by colonization. Consequently, the books and studies published in Russia in the eighteenth century and at the beginning of the nineteenth are of great

5. WOODEN FRONTAL WOLF MASK.

6. MINIATURE HUMAN MASKS OF WOOD.

7. CEREMONIAL HEAD-DRESS.

8. CEREMONIAL HEAD-DRESS. SEE ALSO PLATES 29–31.

9. CEREMONIAL HEAD-DRESS. SEE ALSO PLATE 34.

historical interest. Of equal importance are the collections of North American Indian art of this period in the Leningrad and Moscow museums. Shelikhov, Billings and Sarychev speak of the gifts they were given or the objects they acquired in exchange for other things (1788, 1790–1791). Lisiansky assembled a fine collection during his voyage. He describes how the governor of the colony, Alexander Baranov, once brought him various articles and masks beautifully carved out of wood and decorated in different colours. Other navigators and traders of the Russian American Company also brought home similar objects.

By the middle of the nineteenth century most of the collections of works made by the tribes of Russian America, especially the Tlingits, had been brought together in the Ethnographical Museum of the Academy of Sciences. Although it is often difficult to determine the precise year in which a given object was acquired, it is clear that all these collections were made before the Russian government sold Alaska to the United States in 1867. The only collection made later was built up by the missionary George Chudnovsky in 1890, but this, too, includes objects of a much earlier date which were given to him by the shamans. The major part of the collections can be dated before 1830, being articles collected by the old navigators. One of the most interesting and complete collections of the first half of the nineteenth century was made by the zoologist Voznesensky, who had been sent to America and to Siberia in search of ethnographical material.

At the end of the eighteenth and the beginning of the nineteenth centuries, the Indians, generally known as North-West Coast Indians, were settled along the coastal region from Yakutat Bay in the south-east of Alaska to the mouth of the Columbia River and the innumerable islands, big and small, that sweep down the rugged coast-line, sharply broken up by bays and inlets. To the east a chain of high mountains, covered with thick coniferous

10. CEREMONIAL HEAD-DRESS.

11. FIGURE OF A DANCER.

17

12. HELMET, FACE-PIECE AND ARMOUR.

13. SHAMAN'S WOODEN RATTLE.

14. CARVED WOODEN RATTLE.

15. CARVED WOODEN RATTLE.

forests, cut off the greater part of this region from the vast expanses of the continent. The geographical isolation of the region may well have been the reason for the creation of the distinctive culture of the people living there. This differs greatly from that of the other American Indians.

The North-West Coastal tribes included various physical types speaking different languages, and with different customs and forms of social organization. However, despite this, these groups share a single culture whose main characteristics were quite distinctive.

The differences and peculiarities have made it possible to classify the Coastal Indians into three groups: first, the southern group made up of the Coast Salish and the Nootka tribes; secondly, the central group made up of the Bella-Coola and Kwakiutl tribes; thirdly, the northern group made up of the Tsimshian, Haida and Tlingit tribes.

The origin of the Coastal Indians, the provenance and development of their culture is still a vexed question upon which specialists cannot agree. Since, unfortunately, the necessary archaeological data is lacking, we have not yet been able to go sufficiently far back into the history of these tribes to carry out a scientific study of their origins and of the early stages of their cultural development. Europeans first learnt of their existence in the middle of the eighteenth century, when their social development, culture and art had already reached a fairly high level.

For a living, the tribes depended on the sea. They would usually settle in quiet bays or inlets set back from the coast, near rivers that ensured a supply of fresh water. The villages were made up of one or more linses of teep-roofed houses built of timbers and split planks. The totem of the tribe was painted on the front wall of each house, in which several related families would live. Inside the house was a sleeping platform built around the walls, and here the guests would sit during the big feasts that took place in the winter. The places

16. 'CREST' REPRESENTING A BEAR.

of honour were opposite to the entrance, and the slaves would huddle in the doorway.

In the spring all the villagers would go off together to build shelters of boards and mats which served as the summer camp. Dug-out canoes were used for travelling to the camp, and then for fishing and for hunting at sea. The canoes, hollowed out of the trunk of a red cedar, were long and narrow, differing in construction according to the purpose they were to serve. The ordinary canoes held ten or twelve people, but the big war canoes, which were still being used at the beginning of the nineteenth century, could take up to fifty warriors. The prow and the stern of the canoes were painted, often with the 'crests' of the leader. In his account of a voyage made in 1826, Lütke wrote that the Tlingit canoes were 'so light on the water that no rowing-boat could rival them.'

Food abounded in the sea and the rivers. In the summer the men would go fishing or seal hunting, while the women would collect shellfish, sea-weed, berries and other wild plants and fruit, building up winter stores. Only a few of the northern Indians, living far up the course of the great continental rivers, lived by hunting game, but all the tribes of the different regions, whether they lived in the north or the south, on the coast or inland, did a lively trade in the produce of sea and forest.

The social organization of the Coastal Indians at the end of the eighteenth century and the beginning of the nineteenth is typical of the break-up of the clan system. Each tribe was divided up into an aristocracy, ordinary members of the tribe, and slaves. The highest position was occupied by the hereditary clan leaders who, apart from their tribal prerogatives, also owned the greatest wealth, whether in slaves, canoes, furs or copper.

This society, with its complicated structure, maintained the characteristics of the old clan organization for a long time. The tribes of the northern group were divided into sub-groups or phratries, which no longer existed in the south. The

22

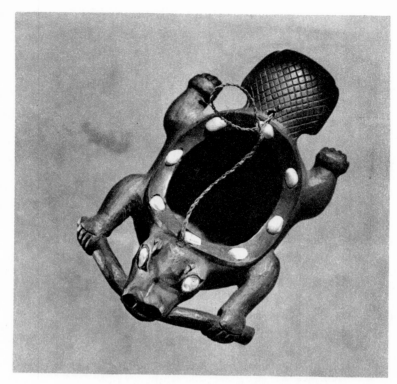

17. WOODEN DISH SHAPED LIKE A SWIMMING BEAVER.

18. WOODEN DISH. LOWER PART IN THE SHAPE OF A BEAVER.

19. MODEL OF A CANOE WITH PADDLERS.

Tlingits had two phratries known as the Raven and the Wolf. The Haidas also had two, the Eagle and the Raven; the Tsimshians four, the Raven, the Eagle, the Wolf and the Bear. Each phratry was composed of several clans, all phratries and clans were named after a totem animal.

By the time the North Pacific coast was colonized it was already difficult to discover any evidence of the animal itself being worshipped; the animal-ancestor had become a mythical man-ancestor, though still closely related to the eponymous animal. The notion of the totem, of the close relationship between man and animal, dominated the social and spiritual life of all the coastal tribes. The totem animals were painted on ceremonial paraphernalia, but they also figured on articles of everyday use. At the same time they served as crests for the leaders.

24

The tribes practised a developed form of animism. The sea, the rivers, the forest, the underground world and the air were full of spirits, good or evil, which took on various forms. Every man had his own spirit protectors and the shamans were the medium of communication with the spirit world. Every shaman had various masks representing different spirits.

The long winter of the North-West Coast was a time of feasts and religious ceremonies, of which the *potlachs* were the most important. At these ceremonies the leaders would distribute presents to boost up their authority. The feasts would last for days on end, accompanied by dance pantomimes that told stories of the genealogical myths. Initiation rites were performed in the winter, as were the ceremonies of the innumerable secret societies which were especially powerful among the Kwakiutl tribes. Whatever different forms they might take, the ceremonies were always bound up with the clan traditions.

20. MODEL OF A CANOE WITH PADDLERS FROM OTHER SIDE.

21. WOODEN MODEL OF A CANOE.

The first explorers were surprised by the solemn ceremonial character of these festivities, as well as by the great beauty of the work on the ceremonial clothes and masks that turned their wearers into the various characters of Indian folklore.

The earliest reports speak of the big wooden houses decorated with carved posts and painted walls, in front of which stood the great totem poles. Travellers were amazed to find that not only were houses and ceremonial objects decorated, but that each household article or utensil, everything that the people used in their everyday life, was a work of art. When Lisiansky visited the North-West Coast in 1805, he wrote: 'Carving and painting can be considered the most important art or handicraft of the local population. Judging from the number of masks and many other carved and painted objects I have seen, we may conclude that every man is an artist. Here you will not find a single tool or dish that is not decorated; this is especially true of boxes and chests whose lids are covered with shells that resemble teeth.'

Every object that the Coastal Indians made was an example of their art. Behind the decoration of each object lay a definite idea that heightened the significance of the article.

From the historical and artistic point of view the most interesting objects are those that have come down to us from the period before the North-West Coastal Indians had met Europeans, and before the latter had influenced the original culture. Most of the objects published in this book belong to this category. Not very long ago even the experts on 'primitive art' would have been surprised at any popular reference to the art of the Coastal Indians of North-West America. African art became well known from 1910 on, while the first scientific work on the culture of the Coastal Indians, written by Leonhard Adam in 1923, did not evoke wide interest among the

22. WOODEN MODEL OF A CANOE.

23. WOODEN PIPE.

24. WOODEN PIPE.

25. SHAMAN'S WOODEN COMB.

26. SHAMAN'S NECKLACE WITH BONE PENDANTS.

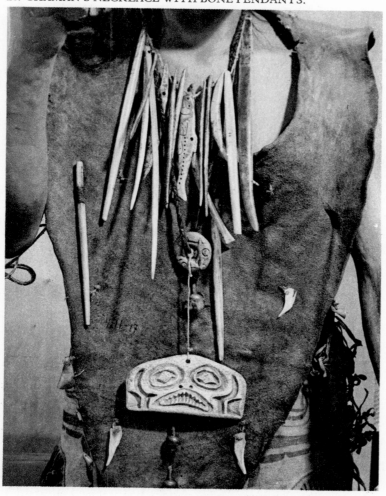

general public. However, in the following years several specialized works on this subject were published and now general works about the cultures of the peoples of Asia, Africa or America include material on the art of the American Coastal Indians. Much valuable material about Indian art, especially in relation to the techniques used and to its social significance, can be found in general ethnographical works on the Indians of North-West America.

Paul Wingert, an expert on the culture of Indians and other people, wrote, 'Typical North-West Coast art is unique among the world's art traditions.' It is certainly the individuality, the virtuosity with which the Indians created each object that makes the art of the Coastal Indians so striking and gives it its exceptional value. Simple household utensils display the extraordinary talent and artistic perception of the men and women who made them. We have already quoted Lisiansky who said that every Indian was an artist, while Viola Garfield called them all 'potential artists.' However, by the end of the eighteenth century there was already specialization among artists and carvers. The Russian navigators Bocharof and Ismailof spoke of this in 1787, and Lütke wrote in 1826 that the carved prow figures of the canoes were made by 'special artists.' The wood carvers achieved great virtuosity and perfection. They decorated great totem poles, masks, ceremonial head-dresses, battle helmets, rattles, halibut hooks, dishes, boxes and chests.

The precision and delicacy of the wood carving is most striking whether it decorates a totem pole or a small rattle. The Indians had a thorough knowledge of the properties of each kind of wood, choosing it carefully to suit the particular article they intended to carve. They used red and yellow cedar, Sitka spruce, yew, alder, maple and American hemlock.

Before the Europeans came to the North-West Coast, the Indians had made their carvings with

27. SHAMAN'S AMULET CARVED FROM A BEAR'S FANG.

tools of stone, shell or beavers' teeth wedged into wooden hafts. By the end of the eighteenth century metal tools were fairly widespread, but although this made the work of carving much easier, the methods used did not change. It has been suggested that the use of metal tools led to the flowering of the art of the Coastal Indians, but this idea is difficult to accept. It would be truer to say that their use led rather to the creation of a larger number of carved objects.

The coming of the new tools did not change the technique born of the experience of many generations. The Indians remained so faithful to their traditions that when they were given axes and knives they carved and shaped them to give them the ancient forms they were used to.

With simple knives and chisels they achieved the most extraordinary results. Besides the fine detail of the work, the art of the Coastal Indians is remarkable for the complexity of form and composition expressed in rounded sculpture, in high and low reliefs and in flat carving.

Wooden sculpture and flat surfaces were often painted. In the sculpture colour was used to bring out the detail and heighten the general artistic effect. Paints were made chiefly from minerals and plants crushed in stone mortars and mixed with salmon roe that had been previously chewed and ground into a soft mass. The artists frequently used a bluish-green colour made of clay containing copper salts. The southern tribes hardly ever used paint on their sculpture, but the Kwakiutls loved very bright paint and developed a particularly rich sense of colour when industrial paints were brought into the region. The northern tribes, especially the Tlingits and Tsimshians, liked to use very soft, restrained tones, although sometimes, when the artist was decorating masks or battle helmets with evil spirits or supernatural beings, he would choose much stronger colours. On flat surfaces the natural colour of the wood or leather was usually taken as the background for a

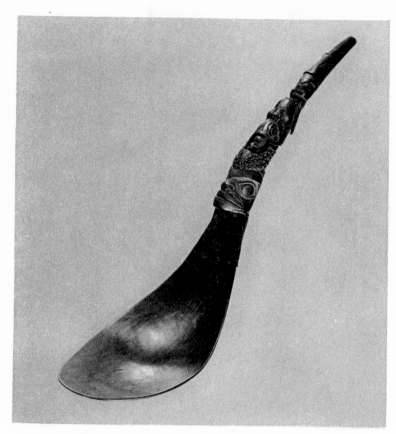

28. GOAT-HORN SPOON. SEE ALSO PLATE 87.

29. GOAT-HORN SPOON.

30. DIPPER MADE OF SHEEP'S HORN.

31. CHILKAT CLOAK. FOR GENERAL VIEW SEE FIG. 32.

design in red and black colours.

Although the art of all the Coastal Indians belonged to a single style, there were certain regional differences. The most perfect art is considered to be that of the northern group, especially the Tlingit and Tsimshian tribes and, to a lesser degree, the Haidas.

The expression of the art of the Coastal Indians is bound up with the use to which most of the objects were put. A definite idea lay behind the decoration of each object and the painting and carving would portray mythological subjects, stressing the close link between man and animal. Carvings nearly always represented men, animals or birds. And of these the favourites were the bear, the wolf, the beaver, the killer whale, the raven, the eagle and the hawk. However, fish are also to be found in the carvings, and even insects, such as the mosquito.

One can sometimes find most realistic carvings showing the complete figure of a man or an animal, but generally the work is considerably stylized. Certain characteristic features of an animal are taken to represent the animal as a whole and turned into a symbol. The masks, helmets and ceremonial head-dresses are typical of this.

Masks in the form of animal heads, of animals with human faces, or of fantastic beings were made by all the Coastal Indians, only varying in details of style. Side by side with the fantastic masks, many of the tribes, especially the Tlingits and the Tsimshians, made very realistic human ones which are remarkable for the refinement of the detail. They are so wonderfully expressive that they sometimes show the beginning of an attempt to express psychological characteristics.

As well as being painted, masks and head-dresses were also inlaid with haliotis shell, decorated with fur, human hair, sea-lion whiskers and feathers. The decoration of the wooden parts of the ceremonial head-dress was particularly magnificent.

Carved rattles were an essential part of dance ceremonies and of the shaman's magic. Most of them, known as 'raven rattles,' represented the raven, the ancestor of one of the Tlingit phratries and the hero of innumerable myths. The superb work on these rattles is one of the finest examples of wood carving. The back of the raven was carved with the figure of a man and the heads of different animals or birds.

Carved dishes, though simple in form, were often very fine and wonderfully expressive, showing various beasts and birds, usually the raven and the beaver.

Ivory and bone carving was less artistic. There were articles made from walrus tusks and bears' fangs (for the shaman's amulets), or from the horn of mountain goat and sheep which was used to fashion small dishes, spoons and ladles. The handles were carved in such complicated patterns that they sometimes looked like miniature totem poles.

The slate carving of the Haida Indians was an art in itself. The argillite slate they used is only found on Queen Charlotte Islands, where the Haidas lived. Many specialists believe that slate carving developed in the middle of the nineteenth century, and in any case these objects were specially made to sell to Europeans. They included small boxes, plates, models of canoes with the paddlers, tiny totem poles, and figures of people (even Europeans).

But the main argillite articles were the pipes, which the Indians themselves never smoked! These pipes were always decorated with an exceedingly complicated combination of figures.

The outer signs of realism had almost completely disappeared, although a realistic expression was implied in the decoration of flat or slightly carved surfaces, such as the fronts of the houses or their inner walls, the tops and sides of chests, dishes or ladles, the sides of canoes, as well as leather receptacles, slat armour and woven fibre

32. CHILKAT CLOAK.

hats. On these articles the ornament of flat carving or painted design was highly stylized. The animal figures were 'split' lengthwise to give them two profiles. This 'splitting' was usually governed by the form of the surface to be decorated. Even more typical was the use of the side space of the main figure to paint or carve ears, wings, eyes or other elements and symbols of the animal portrayed. Eyes were carved or painted so frequently that the ornament of the Coastal Indians was usually known as 'eye ornament.' Each symbol clearly represented the characteristics of the chosen animal. Wingert used a happy term when he spoke of the symbolic abstraction of natural forms. This system of symbolic interpretation was strengthened by the names by which the elements of ornament were known for a very long time. Franz Boas collected a large number of examples at the end of the last century.

All the artistic work of which we have spoken was done by the men. The women's work was very different both as regards the material and the technique used, but it was just as superb in its detail. Their work consisted mostly in weaving articles from straw or fibre or in making cloth. Their baskets and hats woven from split spruce roots were most beautiful, showing ingenuity and elegance. Certain methods of weaving the material led to the creation of their own special designs. Sometimes the patterns were made by weaving dyed vegetable fibres or grasses. Hats were usually decorated with the designs typical of each tribe. On the other hand, the ornamentation of baskets and mats was purely geometrical and bore no relation to myths or beliefs.

The woven stuff of ceremonial robes is particularly well known. This was made from mountain goat hair or from vegetable fibres. A few robes of an earlier type have been preserved, with purely geometrical designs.

Another type was made by one of the Tlingit tribes, called the Chilkats, who have given their

33. FIGURE OF A DANCER.

34. CLOAK. WOVEN FROM THE HAIR OF MOUNTAIN GOATS.

name to the Chilkat cloaks made of white wool patterned in black, yellow andbluish-green. The superb beauty of these blankets lies in the symbolic and stylized ornament ofwhich we have already spoken, that is, the ornament characteristic of the men's art. The men drew or carved the designs on wood and the women weavers copied them. Hence the similarity of the designs which are practically identical, beingrepeated in innumerable combinations. The Chilkat cloaks are the most highly prized.

The household articles and ceremonial objects illustrated in the plates show the high artistic level of the culture of the Coastal Indians of North-West America.

35. SHAMAN'S HEAD-DRESS.

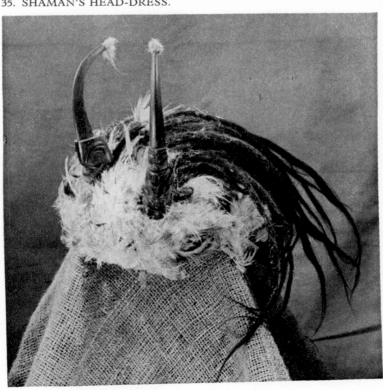

1 - Wooden mask in the form of a human face. From the Lisiansky Collection (?), 1806.
24 cm high, 18 cm wide.   No. 2448-11

2 - Wooden mask of a woman wearing a labret. From an early collection.
21.5 cm high, 16.1 cm wide.   No. 337-2

3 - Shaman's frontal mask of carved wood. The forehead is decorated with wisps of human hair. From the Chudnovsky Collection, 1890. Admiralty Island.
13.5 cm high, 8.7 cm wide.   No. 211-8

4 - Wooden frontal mask in the form of a mosquito. (According to the collector's note.) Eyes and teeth of haliotis shell. Decorated with leather, eagle down, feathers and walrus whiskers. From the Voznesensky Collection, 1839–1845.
50 cm long (including the leather 'wings').   No. 571-20

5 - Wooden frontal wolf mask. It has leather ears with wisps of human hair. From the Voznesensky Collection, 1839–1845.
21 cm long.   No. 2448-2

6 - Miniature human masks of wood, from ceremonial head-dresses. From the Lisiansky Collection, 1806.
(a) 9.5 cm high, 4 cm wide.   No. 536-21
(b) 5 cm high, 3.5 cm wide.   No. 536-21

7, 8 - Ceremonial head-dress. The front part is a wooden mask carved in the shape of a raven and decorated with inlaid haliotis shell. From the P. Doroshin Collection, 1850.
20 cm high, 16.5 cm wide.   No. 2448-19

9 - Ceremonial head-dress. The front part shows two bird masks carved in wood. The eyes, teeth and sides are inlaid with haliotis shell. From an early collection.
22 cm high, 19 cm wide.   No. 2448-21

10 - Ceremonial head-dress. Wood carving, portraying a raven. Wisps of human hair are laid above the eyes. A very unusual piece. From the Museum of the Admiralty Department, 1829.
                                                 No. 2448-18

11 - Figure of a dancer in a cloak (No. 593-26) and a ceremonial head-dress (No. 2448-18). From an early collection.

12 - Helmet, face-piece and armour made of wooden slats. The helmet personifies an evil spirit. From the Voznesensky Collection, 1839-1845. The helmet is 26 cm high (No. 571-14). The wooden face-piece, from an early collection, is 13 cm high in front (No. 2454-22). The armour is made of wooden slats joined by thread. An early acquisition (No. 2454-5).

13 - Shaman's wooden rattle. The other side has a pattern drawn on it. From an early collection.
21 cm long.   No. 5795-38

14 - Carved wooden rattle. It is shaped like a bird with a long, curved neck. The wings are decorated with a carved ornamentation, and the head of a hawk is carved out of the back. The underside also shows a hawk and two curved feet. The work is painted in brown and black. The handle is cylindrical. From the Lisiansky Collection, 1806.
30 cm long.   No. 238-5

15 - Wooden rattle carved in the form of a two-sided human head. It is decorated with a carved 'eye' design painted in brown, blue-green and black. The handle is bound with thongs. From the Lisiansky Collection, 1806.
23 cm long, 13 cm wide. No. 238-3

16 - 'Crest' representing a bear painted on a wooden plank. Old piece, probably presented by G. Shelikhov, 1788.
79 cm long, 24.5 cm wide. No. 2448-30

17 - Wooden dish shaped like a swimming beaver. Eyes of haliotis shell. From an early collection.
6.5 cm high, 16 cm long. No. 2539-19

18 - Wooden dish, the lower part carved in the shape of a beaver. A human face, bent arms and legs are carved on the bottom. From an early collection.
6 cm high, base 9 cm × 6.5 cm. No. 2539-20

19,20 - Model of a canoe with paddlers. The figure on the prow represents a spirit. From the Voznesensky Collection, 1839-1845.
75 cm long, 10 cm high. No. 2520-2

21, 22 - Wooden model of a canoe. An eye design is painted in red and black on the prow and the stern; the middle is painted red. From the Collection of Captain Maksutov[1], 1862–1867. Sitkha Island.
103 cm long, length of the hull 68 cm, 23.5 cm wide, 12 cm high. No. 237-6a

23, 24 - Wooden pipe. The natural light-coloured wood is carved and inlaid with decoratively carved bone. In places it is painted in blue-green and black. It shows a ship, first seen by the Indians in 1840. The upper part represents an animal with a protruding tongue, supporting the pipe, and two sitting men. The back shows a ship's cabin with glass windows and a man inside. The upper part is made of brass plates (according to the inventory). From Captain Maksutov's Collection, 1862–1867.
Acquired in 1868.
32 cm long, 10 cm high. No. 237-13

25 - Shaman's wooden comb. The carving portrays a bear and two human figures. From an early collection.
12 cm high, 9 cm long. No. 2539-30

26 - Shaman's necklace with bone pendants representing his guardian spirits. From the Chudnovsky Collection, 1890. Admiralty Island. No. 211-33

27 - Shaman's amulet carved from a bear's fang. From an early collection.
8.5 cm high. No. 5795-39

28 - Spoon carved from two pieces of goat-horn. It is fastened together with copper bolts. From an early collection.
27 cm long. No. 2539-34

29 - Goat-horn spoon. From the Voznesensky Collection, 1839-1845.
24 cm long. No. 620-22

30 - Dipper made of dark brown wild sheep's horn. Used at funeral ceremonies for eating seal fat in honour of the dead person. The end of the handle is shaped like a beak and carved with the eye ornament. From Captain Maksutov's Collection, 1862–1867.

Overall length 64 cm, length of dipper 29 cm, width 14 cm, height 22 cm.

No. 237/7

31, 32 - Chilkat cloak. From an early collection.

162 cm long, 87 cm wide (not counting the fringe).

No. 5795-17

33 - Figure of a dancer wearing a cloak (No. 5795-17) and a ceremonial head-dress (No. 5795-34). From an early collection.

34 - Cloak. The material is woven from the hair of mountain goats. Brought from the coast by Captain Clark in 1779, (Captain Cook's third expedition).

164 cm long, 106 cm wide.   No. 252-70

35 - Shaman's head-dress (known as Shaman's hair) made of bird's skin and human hair. The front bears two goat horns, the lower part of which has a carved design. From the Chudnovsky Collection, 1890. Admiralty Island.

No. 211-12

---

1 Captain Maksutov was the governor of the Russian North American colonies from 1862 to 1867. In 1868 his collection was presented to the Moscow Public and Rumiantsev Museum. Inventory of the Moscow Public and Rumiantsev Museum. Moscow, 1871, pp 203-204.

BIBLIOGRAPHY

Boas, Franz, *Primitive art*. Oslo, 1927

Davis, Robert T., *Native arts of the Pacific Northwest*. Stanford, 1949

Gunther, Erna, *Northwest Coast Indian art*. Seattle, 1962

Inverarity, Robert B., *Art of the Northwest Coast Indians*. Los Angeles, 1950

Wardwell, Allen, *Yakutat South. Indian art of the Northwest Coast*. Chicago, 1964

Wingert, Paul, 'Tsimshian sculpture.' In: *The Tsimshian: Their arts and music*. New York, 1950

Wingert, Paul, *Primitive art*. New York, 1962

PLATES

I. MASKS

Carved polychrome masks are the most typical of all the works of art of the North American Coastal Indians. They represent totem animals, spirits and mythological beings, and were usually handed down from generation to generation within each clan. However, sometimes they were specially carved for a certain ceremony. The richer families would possess several masks, and the shaman would own a particularly large number.

The masks were mostly used during the totemic or spirit ceremonies held during the winter months. Each secret society had its masks, and mask dances were performed at various social festivities, such as the potlachs. During a ceremony the shaman would change his mask, particularly when healing the sick, according to the spirit he sought to conjure up.

The size and shape of the masks, as well as the way they were worn, varied according to each tribe. The

1

Shaman's wooden mask in the form of a human face. From the G. Chudnovsky Collection, 1890. Admiralty Island.

24 cm high, 17 cm wide.   No. 211-5

Tlingits usually made masks to cover their faces, although frontal masks and head masks existed, as well as tiny masks attached to head-dresses. Masks representing human faces are particularly typical of Tlingit and Tsimshian work. These were sometimes painted or decorated with the crest of the owner's clan. Occasionally we can find a most realistic picture of an animal, but the majority represented a human face accompanied by the symbols used for an animal or a bird. A long straight beak stands for a raven, a sharply hooked one for an eagle, and a hooked one that is turned in to touch the mouth, lips or teeth, represents a hawk. A long muzzle with sharp fangs gives us the wolf, while the bear is shown by a flatter muzzle with sharp fangs and wide nostrils, accompanied by paws with claws. The beaver is shown with his great cutting-teeth, his flat, scaly tail bent under his belly, and is often portrayed with a log between his front paws. Animal ears also appear as symbolic characteristics; they are carved in the front above the eyes, and not at the side, and sometimes have eyes painted on them. Some masks represented fantastic beings, but they, too, usually include traces of the different animals.

2

Wooden mask in the form of a human face. From an early collection.
23 cm high, 18 cm wide.   No. 5795-31

3

Wooden mask in the form of a woman's face with a wooden lip-plug. The eyebrows are made of beaten copper strips, the eyes set with round pieces of wood. From an early collection.
21 cm high, 17.5 cm wide.   No. 2448-10

4

Shaman's wooden mask in the form of a woman's face. Inset mouth. From the Chudnovsky Collection, 1890. Admiralty Island.
21.3 cm high.   No. 211-6

5

Wooden mask in the form of a human face. From
early acquisitions.
19.5 cm high, 16.5 cm wide.   No. 5795-32

6

Shaman's wooden mask in the form of a human face. The eyebrows, eyelids, nostrils and mouth are made of beaten copper strips; the moustache and beard are made of fur. From the Chudnovsky Collection, 1890. Admiralty Island.

28 cm high, 18.5 cm wide.   No. 211-7

7

Shaman's wooden mask in the form of a human face. Another view of Plate 6.

8

Wooden mask showing the moon. From an early collection.
26 cm high, 27 cm wide.   No. 2448-6

9

Shaman's frontal mask of carved wood. It is decorated with feathers and stuck on to a mounting of cloth and birds' skins. From the Chudnovsky Collection, 1890. Admiralty Island.
13.5 cm high, 14 cm wide.   No. 211-3

10

Wooden mask of a mosquito. From an early collection.
21 cm high, 18 cm wide.   No. 2448-13

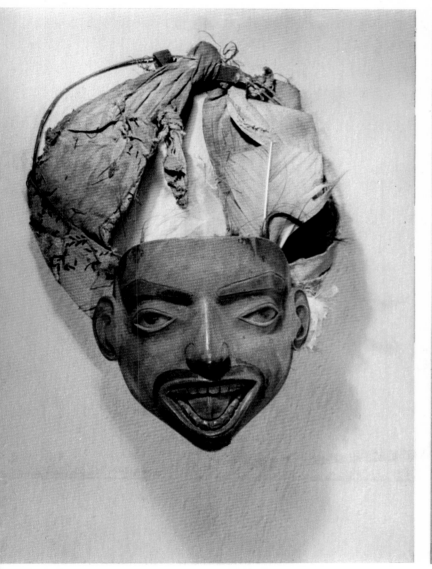 

11

Wooden mask portraying a hawk. The lower lip is inset. The eyes are made of beaten copper strips and wisps of hair, the teeth of shells. From an early collection.

22.5 cm high, 18 cm wide.   No. 5795-26

12

Wooden mask of a bear. From the Voznesensky Collection, 1839–1845.

24 cm high, 18 cm wide.   No. 2448-14

13

Wooden mask, possibly the face-piece of a helmet.
The side fins and tail on the top are made of deerskin. The eyebrows and nostrils are made of copper strips and the teeth of shells. From an early
collection.

17 cm high.   No. 2448-17

14

Wooden mask, possibly the face-piece of a helmet. Another view of Plate 13.

15

Wooden mask. The eyebrows are made of copper strips, the ears, eyes and teeth are inlaid with haliotis shell.

16 cm high.   No. 2448-16

16, 17

Frontal mask. The head of a hawk, with that of an eagle above it, is carved from one piece of wood. The eyebrows are of copper strips; the hawk's head has skin ears. From the Voznesensky Collection, 1839–1845.

17 cm high, profile 19 cm across.   No. 571-19

18

Wooden frontal mask in the form of a mosquito. (According to the collector's note.) Eyes and teeth of haliotis shell. Decorated with leather, eagle down, feathers and walrus whiskers. From the Voznesensky Collection, 1839–1845.
50 cm long (including the leather 'wings').

No. 571-20

19

Wooden frontal mask in the form of a mosquito.
Another view of Plate 18.

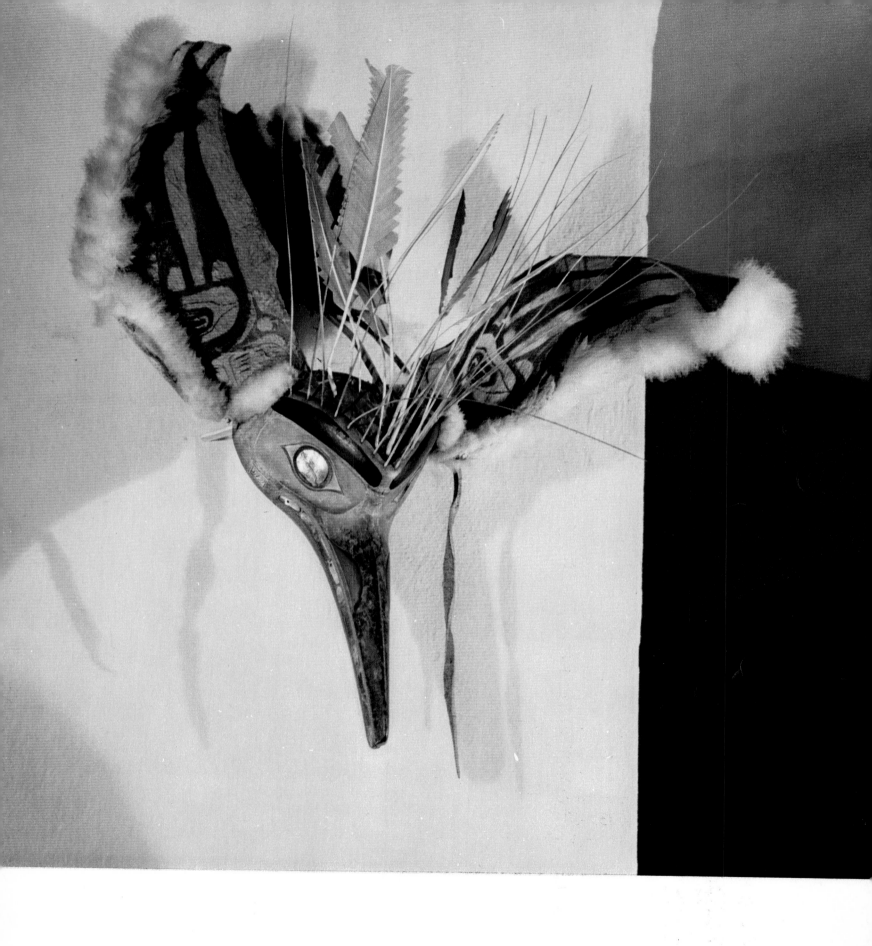

20, 21

This wooden frontal mask probably portrays a killer whale. The side fins are made of leather, the back one of wood. Feathers are stuck on above the eye-brows. From the Voznesensky Collection, 1839–1845.

10 cm high, 16.5 cm long (not counting the 'fins').

No. 2448-3

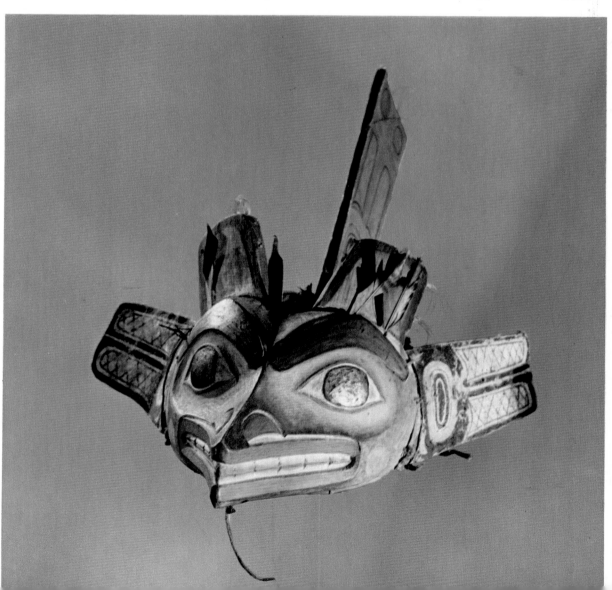

22

Wooden mask of a bear. From an early collection.
34 cm long, 18 cm high.   No. 5795-12

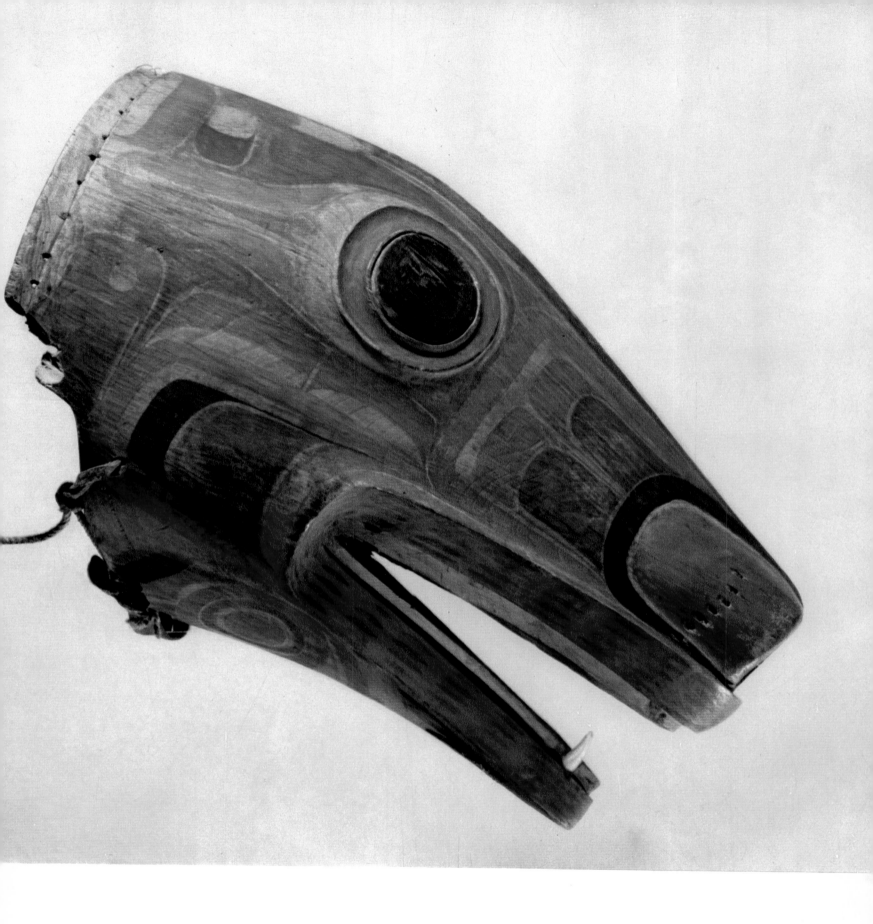

23

Wooden mask of a bear. Another view of Plate 22.

24

Wooden mask carved in the form of a man. Decorated with a drawn and painted ornament in blue-green, black and red. From Captain Maksutov's Collection, 1862–1867.

23 cm high, 17 cm wide.   No. 237-9

25

Wooden mask carved in the form of a man with
moustaches. Painted in green-blue, black and red.
From the Lisiansky Collection, 1806.
24 cm high, 18.5 cm wide.   No. 238-2

26

Wooden mask carved in the form of a man with moustaches. Another view of Plate 25.

27

Wooden mask carved in the form of a woman wearing a labret. Painted ornament in green, pale yellow, red and black. Each side bears thongs to tie it on. From Captain Maksutov's Collection, 1862–1867.

23 cm high, 18 cm wide.   No. 237-8

28

Carved wooden mask (ceremonial head-dress), in the form of a bear's head with a protruding tongue and two front paws. Painted in red, blue, black and white. From the back of the head hang many long braids of human hair; it is decorated with strips of red cloth, fur ears, feathers and eagle down. (Almost all the teeth have been lost and the fur has worn off). From Captain Maksutov's Collection, 1862–1867.

24 cm long, 16 cm wide, 18 cm high.　No. 237-4

II. CEREMONIAL DRESS

Certain forms of head-dress, especially those of the chiefs, bear a very close resemblance to the masks. A chief's head-dress was usually built up on a skeleton of small staves or of whalebone bound with bands of cloth. The upper part of the skeleton was covered with cloth or skins, often the skins of swans with the down. The salient frontlet of these head-dresses was made of a carved wooden plaque, usually inlaid with abalone shell; the top would be decorated with feathers and sea-lions' whiskers, and the sides and back with ermine skins. According to R. Davis, the designs carved on the frontlets represented the crests of the chiefs; others, including E. Gunther, believe that such symbols were rarely used and it is more usually thought that these designs show incidents from the tribal myths.

29

Ceremonial head-dress. The front part is a wooden mask carved in the shape of a raven and decorated with inlaid haliotis shell. From the P. Doroshin Collection, *ca.* 1850.

20 cm high, 16.5 cm wide   No. 2448-19

30

Ceremonial head-dress. Detail of Plate 29.

31

Ceremonial head-dress. Detail of Plate 29.

32

Ceremonial head-dress. The front part is made of carved wood decorated with shell. It portrays a sitting beaver. From an early collection.
21 cm high, 15 cm wide.   No. 2448-20

33

Ceremonial head-dress. Detail of Plate 32.

34

Ceremonial head-dress. The front part shows two bird masks carved in wood. The eyes, teeth and sides are inlaid with haliotis shell. From an early collection.

22 cm high, 19 cm wide.   No. 2448-21

35

The front part of a ceremonial head-dress. Wood carving, showing a stylized raven. Of unknown origin. Damaged.

22 cm high, 15.5 cm wide.   No. 4291-2

III. ARMOUR

If they were preparing to go into battle, either against another tribe or against Europeans, the Tlingits would put on their war-dress. This consisted of elk-skin shirts and armour made of wooden slats intertwined with threads of plaited sinews. The various pieces of slat armour were joined into a whole by leather belts or bands. On the breast, and sometimes on the back, the tribe's totem or protecting spirit would be painted in the space left free of the plaited threads. The warrior's head and neck was protected by a helmet and a kind of visor which was put on round the neck and fastened at the back. It was hollowed out inside to give space for the nose and had tiny round eyeholes and breathing holes. The visor would be covered with carving and sometimes painted or decorated with haliotis shell.

The heavy wooden helmets that protected the upper part of the head were also decorated with totems

36

The front part of a ceremonial head-dress. Another view of Plate 35.

37

Helmet and mask carved from one piece of wood. Tiny human masks are attached to the corners of the mouth. From an early collection.
23 cm high. No. 2454-12

or spirits, and were often realistic portrayals of the heads of animals or birds. Sometimes they were covered with animal skins. One interesting helmet representing a bear's head is completely covered with sealskin. Many helmets were decorated with masks which were actually carved out of the same piece of wood as the helmet.

Both Alexander Baranof (in 1792) and Admiral Lütke (in 1826) wrote that the Tlingit warriors wore complete battle equipment, which means that helmets with masks were still, at that time, part of their war dress. However, gradually, as battles became less and less frequent, the mask-helmets became part of the ceremonial head-dress. In one of his log-books written in 1840, Voznesensky called these mask-helmets used in the performance of ceremonial dances 'head-masks.'

38

Helmet and mask carved from one piece of wood. The mask portrays 'a high-born man' (collector's note). The eyes and teeth are made of haliotis shell. From the Voznesensky Collection, 1839-1845.

2.05 cm high.   No. 571-17

39

Helmet and mask carved from one piece of wood.
Another view of Plate 38.

40

Helmet and mask carved from one piece of wood. The mask portrays an evil spirit. It is decorated with human hair and pieces of skin, while the eyes and teeth are made of haliotis shell. From the Voznesensky Collection, 1839–1845.

24.5 cm high.   No. 571-15

41

Wooden helmet (a) on a carved neck-piece (b).
From an early collection.
(a) 22.5 cm high, 34.5 cm long.   No. 633-8
(b) 16 cm high (in the middle), 4 cm high (at the
sides).   No. 5795-9

42

Wooden helmet. Teeth of shells; moustache and
beard of fur. Acquired from the Museum of the
Admiralty Department in 1829.
22.5 cm high (at the largest part), 34.5 cm long.
                                           No. 633-8

43, 44

Helmet and mask portraying an eagle. It is carved
from one piece of wood, and has shell teeth. From
an early collection.
24 cm high.   No. 2452-11

45

Helmet and mask portraying a hawk. (Collector's note.) It is carved from one piece of wood. The eyes and teeth are made of haliotis shell. From the Voznesensky Collection, 1839–1845.

21 cm high.   No. 571-16

46

Wooden helmet portraying an eagle. Eyes of haliotis shell. From the Voznesensky Collection, 1839-1845.

17.8 cm high.   No. 571-18

47, 48

Wooden helmet in the form of a stylized mountain
goat. Shell teeth. From an early collection.
24 cm high. No. 2454-13

49

Wooden helmet in the form of a goat. From an early collection.
24.5 cm high.   No. 2454-18

50

Wooden helmet shaped like a seal's head. From an early collection.
20 cm high.   No. 2454-16

51

Helmet in the form of a bear's head. It is hollowed
out of wood and covered with sealskin. Shell teeth.
From an early collection.
21ᵣcm high.   No. 5795-10

52

Wooden visor with a carved design. It is encrusted with small pieces of shell. From an early collection.

14 cm high (from the front).   No. 2454-21

53

Wooden visor with a carved design. Detail of Plate 52.

IV. RATTLES

The wooden rattles are always remarkable for the delicacy of their carving which is most realistic in style. They were usually painted to bring out each detail. The rattles were made of two pieces of wood hollowed out, and filled with pebbles. They were bound with threads of sinew or vegetable fibre wound round the handle.

There were two types of rattles, one round or oval, usually known as the shaman's rattle, the other called the raven or chief's rattle. The latter type usually represented a raven, but sometimes a cormorant or a crane. The back of the rattle would be covered with intricate carving representing the figure of a man, usually reclining, and the heads of different animals or birds. The lower part of the rattle would most often represent the head of a hawk and sometimes birds' claws.

The shaman's rattles were used for healing ceremonies and for dances; the Tlingit shamans also used raven rattles. The chiefs used their rattles when speaking at ceremonies.

54, 55

Carved wooden rattle. It is shaped like a raven with the figure of a shaman on its back. The head of a hawk is carved on the lower part. From the Voznesensky Collection, 1839–1845.

28 cm long.   No. 620-20a

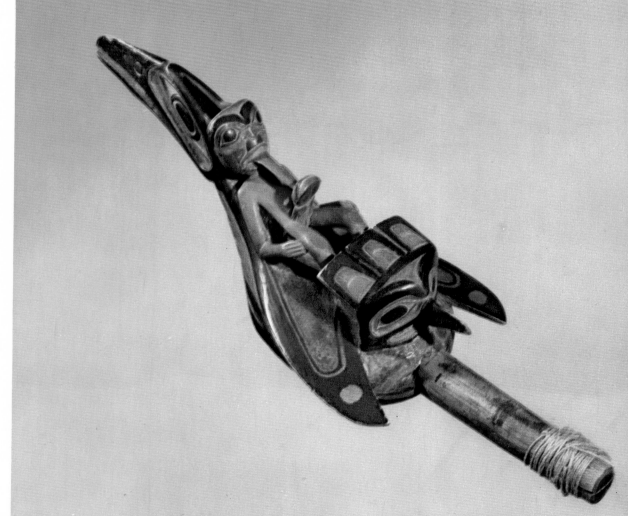

56

Carved wooden rattle in the form of a crane. The back is decorated with two human figures and the head of a mountain goat. From the Voznesensky Collection, 1839–1845.

33 cm long.   No. 2448-25

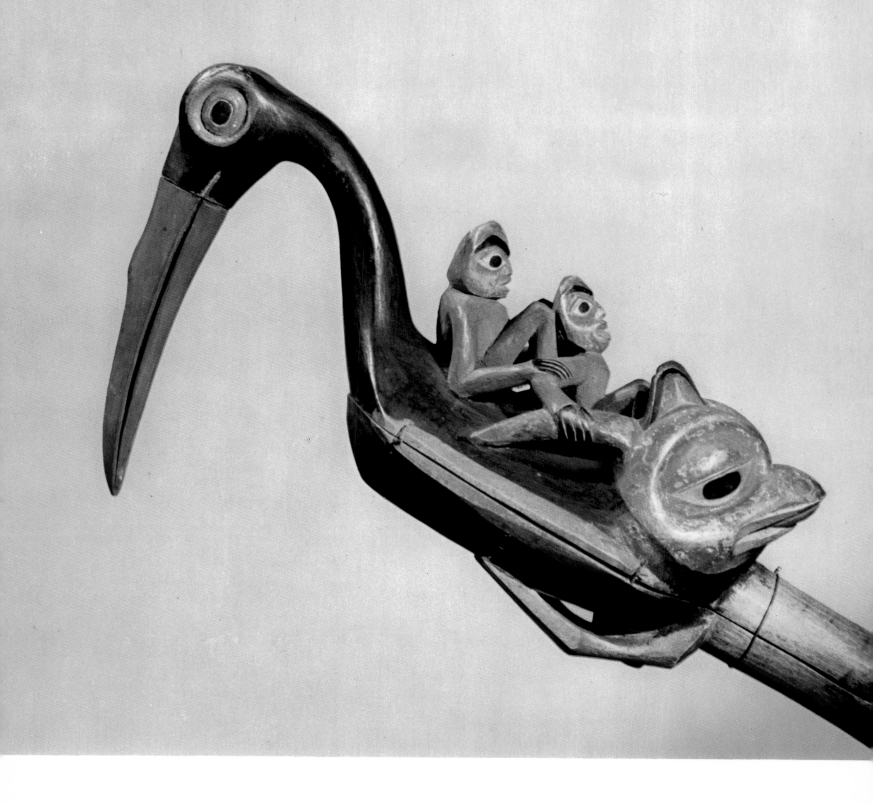

57

Wooden rattle in the form of a crane or a cormorant. The back is decorated with the head of a mountain goat, between whose horns are carved two human figures and an animal. The lower part is carved with webbed feet and a hawk's head. From the Chudnovsky Collection, 1890. Admiralty Island.

29 cm long.   No. 211-2

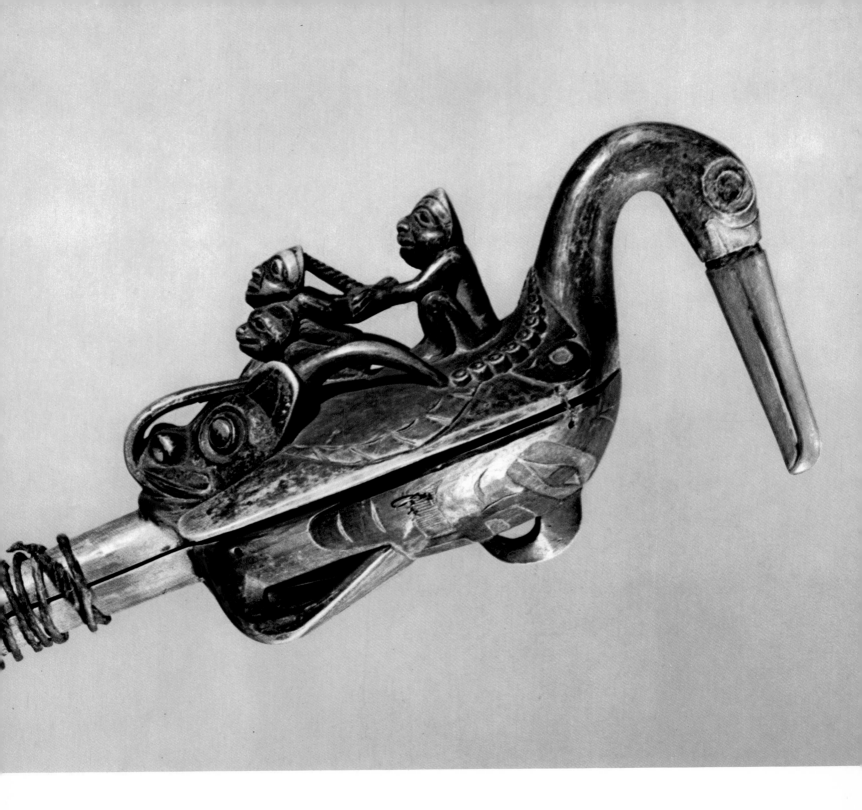

58

Wooden rattle in the form of a crane or a cormorant. Another view of Plate 57.

59, 60

Carved wooden rattle in the form of a raven. The
raven bears on its back a man with a frog on his
knees and its tongue in his mouth. Below is a bird's
head supporting the frog. The raven's wings are
decorated with the eye design. The lower part is
carved into the head of a hawk. It is painted in
brown, blue-green and black. The handle is bound
with thongs. Damaged. One wing is broken.
From the Lisiansky Collection, 1806.
32 cm long.   No. 238-4

V. DISHES

The carved wooden dishes were of many shapes and kinds, depending on the use for which the article was intended. Oil dishes, food dishes or bowls for storing food were not usually painted but were decorated with carving and the edges inlaid with various shells. Many dishes were carved in the form of animals, especially the beaver and the raven.

Dry goods and other objects were kept in more simple dishes, in boxes of different sizes, all carved and painted.

The chests used to store clothes and masks are particularly finely ornamented with carving in low relief.

61, 62

Wooden oil-dish. The edges are inlaid with shells and the front panel shows a beaver. From the Chudnovsky Collection, 1890. Admiralty Island. 16 cm high, 28.6 cm long, 25.3 cm wide.

No. 211-23/2

63

Wooden oil-dish. The edges are inlaid with shells. The carving shows a beaver whose eyes and nostrils are made of haliotis shell. From the Doroshin Collection, *ca*. 1850.
12 cm high, 20 cm long, 18.5 cm wide.

No. 337-18

64, 65

Wooden oil-dish in the form of a beaver. The top
is inlaid with shell. From an early collection.
8 cm high, 28 cm long.   No. 2539-18

66

Wooden oil-dish in the form of a beaver. Edges are inlaid with shell. From an early collection. 12 cm high, 27 cm long.   No. 2539-17

67

Wooden oil-dish in the form of a beaver. Another view of Plate 66.

68

Wooden dish carved in the form of a raven with a
human face at the tail end. From an early collection.
41.5 cm high, 15.5 cm long (face 12 × 6.3 cm).

No. 2539-15

69

Wooden dish carved in the form of a raven.
Another view of Plate 68.

70

Wooden dish. The edges are inlaid with birds'
bones. From an early collection.
Maximum height: 11.5 cm, 23.5 cm wide.

No. 2539-22

71

Wooden dish with decorative carving. The edges
are inlaid with shell. From an early collection.
12 cm high.   No. 2539-21

VI. WOOD CARVINGS

Wood was the principal material available for the Coastal Indians. From it they made their beautiful canoes. The models show how they were shaped and painted with typical ornament, usually showing the chief's totem. Lütke tells us that the big canoes of the Tlingits were known by special names, such as Sun, Moon, Whale, Beaver, Eagle, *and so on, and each canoe had the appropriate figure carved on the prow.*

Other smaller objects of wood were made with equal care and skill. The halibut hooks are particularly fascinating. They were made of two pivots on to

72

Halibut fishing hook. It is carved in the form of a raven's head. From an early collection.
30 cm long.   No. 2539-2

73

Halibut fishing hook. The carving represents octopus suckers and two human figures. From an early collection.
39.5 cm long.   No. 2539-3

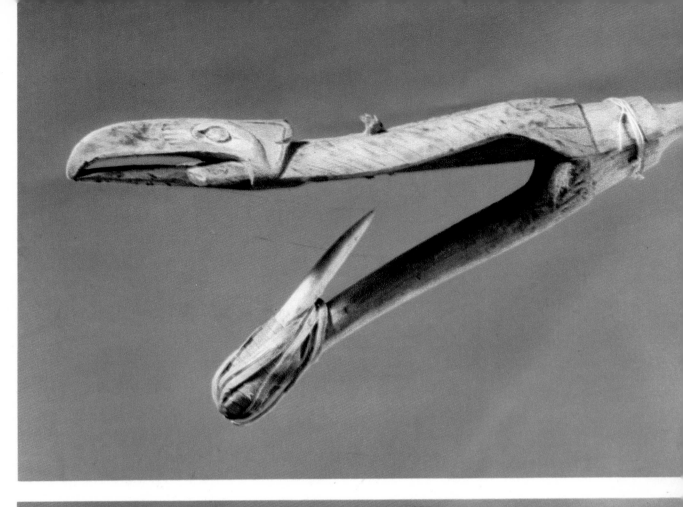

which sharp teeth of bone or iron were stuck, the whole carved into the shape of a symbolic figure.

Wooden combs were also carved along the top with the figures of animals or people.

The 'crest' of the clan or family was carved in the form of a figure standing beside a house, or painted on the sides of the dwellings and on wooden boards.

A painted decoration of reds and red-browns usually covered the flat surfaces of boxes and chests, the sides of small objects and spoons.

74

Carved wooden figure of a mythical being. According to E. Gunther the figure is difficult to interpret; from the design she believes it is unlikely to be the product of the Tlingit culture (personal communication). From the collection of the Museum of the Admiralty Department, 1829.
71–75 cm high.   No. 633-31

75

Carved wooden figure of a mythical being. Another view of Plate 74.

76

Carved wooden figure of a mythical being. Detail of Plate 74.

77

Carved comb made of polished brown wood, showing a bear sitting on a frog, holding a baby in its teeth. The eyes and ears are made of shell incrustations. From Captain Maksutov's Collection, 1862–1867.

15.5 cm long, 7.5 cm wide.   No. 237-11

78

Wooden storage chest with lid.
For detail see Plate 80.

79

Long wooden pipe, carved in the form of a monster's head. The front portrays a bear (?) and the back a hawk. The sides are covered with eye design carvings. The bottom is covered with nine small carved heads, a human one in the centre, frogs' heads and feet at the sides, and behind them other human heads, three on each side. The pipe is painted with a black design. The tube is edged with copper plates. Captain Maksutov's Collection, 1862–1867.

21 cm long, 13 cm wide, 14 cm high.   No. 237-12a

80

Wooden storage chest with lid. Decorated with carving of stylized human faces and the eye design, painted in brown, blue-green and black. Inlaid with shells. From Captain Maksutov's Collection, 1862–1867.

66 cm long, 42 cm wide, 45 cm high.

No. 237-14abcd

81

Wooden storage chest with lid. Detail of Plate 80.

VII. SHAMANISTIC AMULETS

The Indians also used their wood-carving tools to carve various objects of bone, horn, bears' teeth or ivory. These were usually the shaman's amulets. At times the charms were inlaid with haliotis shell. They represented spirits and would be attached to necklaces or sewn on to clothes. The Tlingits carved 'soul catchers' from the shin bones of deer or elks, for they believed that the shamans could use this instrument to catch the soul that was flying away from a man and make it return into his body.

82

Shaman's carved bone amulet. Damaged; perhaps a bear with the head broken off. From the Chudnovsky Collection, 1890. Admiralty Island. 7.5 cm long.   No. 211-24

83

Possibly a shaman's amulet carved from a bear's fang. From the Chudnovsky Collection, 1890. Admiralty Island.

9.5 cm high.   No. 211-32

84

Shaman's amulet carved from a bear's fang. From an early collection.
8 cm high.   No. 5795-45

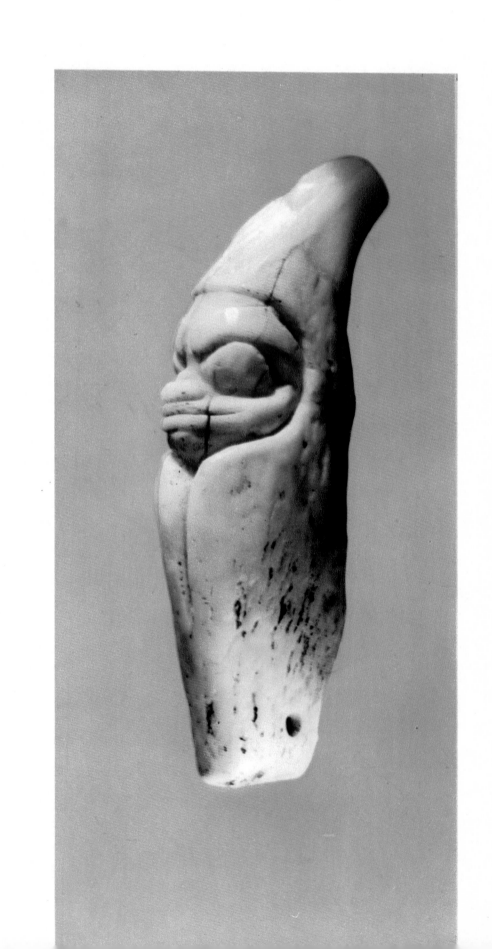

85

Shaman's 'soul-catcher' carved from bone. From an early collection.

10 cm long.   No. 5795-47

86

Bone amulet of an eagle's head. From the Chudnovsky Collection, 1890. Admiralty Island.
11 cm long.   No. 211-25

VIII. HOUSEHOLD OBJECTS

Spoons used at ceremonial feasts were made out of the horns of mountain goats and sheep. The shining black horn of the mountain goats was used to make smaller spoons or the handles for the bigger spoons that were carved from rams' horns. The handles were heavily carved in the shape of figures somewhat like those on totem poles.

The few objects of stone to be found in the museums are of particular interest. Stone was used for tools such as mauls for driving piles into the beds of rivers and wedges for splitting trunks into planks. It was also used for mortars, pestles, and dishes, for small charms, and for figures representing men, birds or animals.

Despite the difficulty of working stone, these objects are remarkable for their artistic qualities. Even on working tools we find, however simplified, a fairly expressive representation of the heads of men or animals. Mortars and dishes were sometimes carved in the form of the wooden dishes.

The artist who made the human mask now in the Musée de l'Homme in Paris, achieved an amazing degree of expression.

87

Spoon. It is carved from two pieces of goat-horn fastened together with copper bolts. From an early collection.

27 cm long.   No. 2539-34

88

Stone hammer. One side of the head is carved, possibly in the shape of a frog. From the Lisiansky Collection, 1806.

18 cm × 11 cm.   No. 563-3

IX. COSTUMES AND HEAD-DRESSES

It was the women who made the clothes, whether they were for everyday use or for the great ceremonies. They used various techniques to weave hats of split spruce roots, decorating them with the painted designs usually connected with the owner's totem.

The finest examples of their work are to be found in the cloaks they wove from mountain goat hair and from vegetable fibres. They had not even the simplest looms; the warp threads were hung from a cross-beam strengthened with two vertical poles. Various patterns were customary, such as squares placed one on the other, combinations of zig-zags, and so on. They were usually carried out in black or brown wool. The Chilkat cloaks have become famous for the complicated style of decoration which the women copied from designs that the men made on boards.

89

Hat made by weaving split spruce roots. Decorated with painted design. From the Voznesensky Collection, 1839–1845.

16.5 cm high, diameter 49 cm.   No. 620-19

Apart from cloaks, the women also wove aprons, on to which they sometimes sewed a second skin apron.

The women made the leather for shirts, aprons and leggings which they decorated with fringes hung with birds' beaks; they also drew designs on them in black, red and greenish paint. Smaller objects, such as pouches, were sometimes embroidered with porcupine quills.

90

Hat made by weaving split spruce roots. Another view of Plate 89.

91

Hats made by weaving split spruce roots, with painted ornament. A chief's hat (a) and a hat decorated with beads and seals' whiskers (b). From the Voznesensky Collection, 1839–1845.

(a) 24 cm high, 38 cm in diameter.   No. 593-34
(b) 12.5 cm high, 37 cm in diameter. No. 5795-22

92

Spruce-root hats. Decorated with a painted design of stylized birds. From an early collection.
(a) 10 cm high, 42.5 cm in diameter.

No. 2520-14 (above)

(b) 9.5 cm high, 33.5 cm in diameter.

No. 2520-27 (below)

93

Chilkat cloak. From an early collection.
162 cm long, 87 cm wide (not counting the fringe).

No. 5795-17

94, 95

Dancing apron. The under apron of soft leather, over apron of Chilkat cloth. Puffins' bills are hung on the fringe as pendants. From the Voznesensky Collection, 1839–1845.

(a) 120 cm wide, 69 cm long (with the fringe)
(b) 91 cm wide, 14–39 cm long.   No. 593-28

96

Sleeveless war-shirt of deerskin. The front is decorated with a painted design. From the Voznesensky Collection, 1839–1845.
88 cm long (not counting the fringe).

No. 2454-10

97, 98

Shaman's apron of soft deerskin. It is decorated with painted and beaded design. From an early collection.

105 cm × 46 cm.   No. 5795-14

99

Shaman's deerskin pouch. The design is embroidered in porcupine quills and portrays a bear.
From an early collection.
17 cm long, 21 cm wide.   No. 2520-1

100

Double-edged iron dagger. From the Voznesensky
Collection, 1839–1845.
53 cm long.   No. 571-74

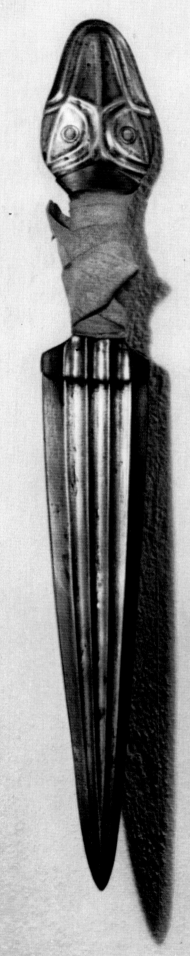

101

Family 'crest' painted on leather. From an early collection (perhaps acquired by G. Shelikhov, 1788).
49 cm long, 24 cm wide.   No. 2448-29

102

Double-edged iron dagger. Eyes are of haliotis shell. Acquired in 1867 by the Russian Geographical Society.
54 cm long.   No. 236-4ab

103

Shaman's fringed leather apron. The design, painted in black, white, yellow and dark green, shows symbolic ornamentation and a stylized human face in the centre. From Captain Maksutov's Collection, 1862–1867.

64 cm long with fringe, 44 cm wide (without fringe).   No. 237-2

104

Breast-plate made of soft deerskin, with separate wing pieces at the sides, and thong strings. Painted in red, green and black with the eye design. In the centre a stylized face. Presented by the Russian Geographical Society to the Ethnographical Exhibition of 1867, organized in Moscow by the Society of Lovers of Natural History, Anthropology and Ethnography.

70 cm overal length, 84 cm overall width.

40 cm long (upper wings), 35 cm wide.

30 cm long (lower wings), 34 cm wide.

No. 236-3

105

Breast-plate made of soft deerskin. Detail of Plate 104.

106, 107 ▶

Carved wooden figure of a shaman. Long black strands of human hair are attached to the head. The figure is fully dressed with a breast-plate, apron and cloak of brown-black deerskin decorated with a design of human faces, the figure of a man and the eye pattern. On the head is a wooden hat with three little cylinders on which the eye design is painted in red. Round the neck is a necklace of bone drops which is part of the shamans' paraphenalia. From Captain Maksutov's Collection, 1862–1867.

23 cm high, including hat.   No. 237/15